F·R·I·E·N·D·S

THE OFFICIAL
RECIPE JOURNAL

THIS RECIPE JOURNAL BELONGS TO:

_____

Life—and food—is better with friends! There's a recipe for everyone, whether you're a professional chef like Monica, prefer faceless foods like Phoebe, enjoy milk you can chew like Chandler, have a truly unique English trifle recipe like Rachel, crave Moist Maker sandwiches like Ross, or just love all food like Joey.

This journal is for you to keep a record of the delicious recipes you've made, shared, or received from the kitchens of your friends. With prompts to remind you of each recipe's origin, and space to jot down memories, this book will become a treasured keepsake of time spent and memories made with friends over a meal. And, throughout this book's pages, the Friends have left a few recipes of their own for you to enjoy!

Breakfasts AND Breads

Scones . . . MY Scones

2 cups all-purpose flour, plus more
 for dusting
3 tablespoons sugar
2½ teaspoons baking powder
¼ teaspoon sea salt
½ cup (4 ounces) cold unsalted
 butter, cut into chunks, plus
 more for serving
½ cup dried fruit or other add-ins,
 such as dried currants, crystalized
 ginger, or dried cherries
1 cup heavy cream

Line a baking sheet with parchment paper. In a bowl, sift together the flour, sugar, baking powder, and salt. Using a pastry blender or 2 knives, cut the butter into the flour mixture just until the mixture forms large, coarse crumbs the size of peas. Add the dried fruit or other add-ins of your choice. Pour the cream over the dry ingredients and stir with a fork or rubber spatula just until combined.

Turn the dough out onto a lightly floured work surface and pat into a circle about ½ inch thick. Using a 2½-inch biscuit cutter, cut out as many rounds of the dough as possible. Gather up the scraps, knead briefly, and continue patting and cutting out to make 8 scones. Alternately, use a sharp knife to cut into 8 wedges. Place each scone 1 inch apart on the prepared baking sheet.

Bake until golden brown, 17 to 20 minutes. Transfer to a wire rack and let cool slightly. Serve warm or at room temperature.

"**My scone!**" —Joey "**My scone!**" —Phoebe, Ross, and Joey

"**Okay, I do not sound like that.
That is so not true.**" —Chandler

· BREAKFASTS & BREADS RECIPES ·

1. Scones...MY Scones

2.

3.

4.

5.

6.

7.

8.

9.

10.

11.

12.

13.

14.

15.

16.

17.

18.

19.

20.

Recipe:

FROM THE KITCHEN OF: _____

· NOTES / TIPS ·

SERVINGS:

PREP / COOK TIME:

PREHEAT OVEN:

· INGREDIENTS ·

· DIRECTIONS ·

_____

_____

_____

_____

_____

_____

_____

_____

_____

_____

_____

_____

_____

_____

_____

About my Friend

How we met: _____

_____

How long we've known each other: _____

What's special about this recipe: _____

_____

A favorite memory with my friend: _____

_____

_____

My favorite thing about my friend: _____

_____

Recipe:

FROM THE KITCHEN OF: _____

· NOTES / TIPS ·

SERVINGS:

PREP / COOK TIME:

PREHEAT OVEN:

· INGREDIENTS ·

· DIRECTIONS ·

_____

_____

_____

_____

_____

_____

_____

_____

_____

_____

_____

_____

_____

_____

_____

About my Friend

How we met: _____

_____

How long we've known each other: _____

What's special about this recipe: _____

_____

A favorite memory with my friend: _____

_____

_____

My favorite thing about my friend: _____

_____

Recipe: _____

FROM THE KITCHEN OF: _____

• NOTES / TIPS •

_____
_____
_____
_____
_____
_____
_____

SERVINGS:

PREP / COOK TIME:

PREHEAT OVEN:

• INGREDIENTS •

_____   _____
_____   _____
_____   _____
_____   _____
_____   _____
_____   _____
_____   _____
_____   _____

· DIRECTIONS ·

_____

_____

_____

_____

_____

_____

_____

_____

_____

_____

_____

_____

_____

_____

_____

_____

About my Friend

How we met: _____

_____

How long we've known each other: _____

What's special about this recipe: _____

_____

A favorite memory with my friend: _____

_____

_____

My favorite thing about my friend: _____

_____

Recipe: _____

FROM THE KITCHEN OF: _____

SERVINGS:

PREP / COOK TIME:

PREHEAT OVEN:

· NOTES / TIPS ·

· INGREDIENTS ·

· DIRECTIONS ·

_____
_____
_____
_____
_____
_____
_____
_____
_____
_____
_____
_____
_____

About my Friend

How we met: _____
_____

How long we've known each other: _____

What's special about this recipe: _____
_____

A favorite memory with my friend: _____
_____
_____

My favorite thing about my friend: _____
_____

Recipe: _____

FROM THE KITCHEN OF: _____

· NOTES / TIPS ·

_____
_____
_____
_____
_____
_____
_____

SERVINGS:

PREP / COOK TIME:

PREHEAT OVEN:

· INGREDIENTS ·

_____   _____
_____   _____
_____   _____
_____   _____
_____   _____
_____   _____

"Bagels and donuts. Round food for every mood."

—*Chandler*

· DIRECTIONS ·

_____

_____

_____

_____

_____

_____

_____

_____

_____

_____

_____

_____

_____

About my Friend

How we met: _____

_____

How long we've known each other: _____

What's special about this recipe: _____

_____

A favorite memory with my friend: _____

_____

_____

My favorite thing about my friend: _____

_____

Recipe:

FROM THE KITCHEN OF: _____

· NOTES / TIPS ·

SERVINGS:

PREP / COOK TIME:

PREHEAT OVEN:

· INGREDIENTS ·

· DIRECTIONS ·

_____

_____

_____

_____

_____

_____

_____

_____

_____

_____

_____

_____

_____

_____

About my Friend

How we met: _____

_____

How long we've known each other: _____

What's special about this recipe: _____

_____

A favorite memory with my friend: _____

_____

_____

My favorite thing about my friend: _____

_____

Recipe:

FROM THE KITCHEN OF:

SERVINGS:

PREP / COOK TIME:

PREHEAT OVEN:

· NOTES / TIPS ·

· INGREDIENTS ·

· DIRECTIONS ·

_____
_____
_____
_____
_____
_____
_____
_____
_____
_____
_____
_____
_____
_____

About my Friend

How we met: _____
_____

How long we've known each other: _____

What's special about this recipe: _____
_____

A favorite memory with my friend: _____
_____
_____

My favorite thing about my friend: _____
_____

Recipe: _____

FROM THE KITCHEN OF: _____

· NOTES / TIPS ·

SERVINGS:

PREP / COOK TIME:

PREHEAT OVEN:

· INGREDIENTS ·

· DIRECTIONS ·

_____
_____
_____
_____
_____
_____
_____
_____
_____
_____
_____
_____
_____
_____
_____

About my Friend

How we met: _____
_____

How long we've known each other: _____

What's special about this recipe: _____
_____

A favorite memory with my friend: _____
_____

_____

My favorite thing about my friend: _____
_____

Recipe: _____

FROM THE KITCHEN OF: _____

· NOTES / TIPS ·

SERVINGS:

PREP / COOK TIME:

PREHEAT OVEN:

_____
_____
_____
_____
_____
_____
_____
_____

· INGREDIENTS ·

_____   _____
_____   _____
_____   _____
_____   _____
_____   _____
_____   _____
_____   _____
_____   _____
_____   _____

· DIRECTIONS ·

_____
_____
_____
_____
_____
_____
_____
_____
_____
_____
_____
_____
_____
_____
_____

About my Friend

How we met: _____
_____

How long we've known each other: _____
What's special about this recipe: _____
_____

A favorite memory with my friend: _____
_____
_____

My favorite thing about my friend: _____
_____

Recipe: _____

FROM THE KITCHEN OF: _____

· NOTES / TIPS ·

_____

SERVINGS: _____

_____

PREP / COOK TIME: _____

_____

PREHEAT OVEN: _____

_____

_____

_____

· INGREDIENTS ·

_____	_____
_____	_____
_____	_____
_____	_____
_____	_____
_____	_____

"Oh come on. Nobody likes two different kinds of eggs equally. You like one better than the other and I wanna know which."

—Joey

· DIRECTIONS ·

_____

_____

_____

_____

_____

_____

_____

_____

_____

_____

_____

_____

_____

_____

About my Friend

How we met: _____

_____

How long we've known each other: _____

What's special about this recipe: _____

_____

A favorite memory with my friend: _____

_____

_____

My favorite thing about my friend: _____

_____

Recipe:

FROM THE KITCHEN OF: _____

SERVINGS:

PREP / COOK TIME:

PREHEAT OVEN:

· NOTES / TIPS ·

· INGREDIENTS ·

· DIRECTIONS ·

_____

_____

_____

_____

_____

_____

_____

_____

_____

_____

_____

_____

_____

_____

About my Friend

How we met: _____

_____

How long we've known each other: _____

What's special about this recipe: _____

_____

A favorite memory with my friend: _____

_____

_____

My favorite thing about my friend: _____

_____

Recipe:

FROM THE KITCHEN OF: _____

· NOTES / TIPS ·

SERVINGS:

PREP / COOK TIME:

PREHEAT OVEN:

· INGREDIENTS ·

· DIRECTIONS ·

_____
_____
_____
_____
_____
_____
_____
_____
_____
_____
_____
_____
_____
_____

About my Friend

How we met: _____
_____

How long we've known each other: _____

What's special about this recipe: _____
_____

A favorite memory with my friend: _____
_____
_____

My favorite thing about my friend: _____
_____

Recipe:

FROM THE KITCHEN OF: _____

· NOTES / TIPS ·

SERVINGS:

PREP / COOK TIME:

PREHEAT OVEN:

· INGREDIENTS ·

· DIRECTIONS ·

_____

_____

_____

_____

_____

_____

_____

_____

_____

_____

_____

_____

_____

_____

About my Friend

How we met: _____

_____

How long we've known each other: _____

What's special about this recipe: _____

_____

A favorite memory with my friend: _____

_____

_____

_____

My favorite thing about my friend: _____

_____

Recipe:

FROM THE KITCHEN OF: _____

· NOTES / TIPS ·

SERVINGS:

PREP / COOK TIME:

PREHEAT OVEN:

· INGREDIENTS ·

· DIRECTIONS ·

_____
_____
_____
_____
_____
_____
_____
_____
_____
_____
_____
_____
_____
_____

About my Friend

How we met: _____
_____

How long we've known each other: _____

What's special about this recipe: _____
_____

A favorite memory with my friend: _____
_____
_____

My favorite thing about my friend: _____
_____

Recipe:

FROM THE KITCHEN OF:

SERVINGS:

PREP / COOK TIME:

PREHEAT OVEN:

· NOTES / TIPS ·

· INGREDIENTS ·

"Please, take your time. It's an important decision, not like say, I don't know, deciding to marry someone. This is about a muffin.

—Ross

· DIRECTIONS ·

_____

_____

_____

_____

_____

_____

_____

_____

_____

_____

_____

_____

_____

_____

About my Friend

How we met: _____

_____

How long we've known each other: _____

What's special about this recipe: _____

_____

A favorite memory with my friend: _____

_____

_____

My favorite thing about my friend: _____

_____

Recipe:

FROM THE KITCHEN OF:

SERVINGS:

PREP / COOK TIME:

PREHEAT OVEN:

· NOTES / TIPS ·

· INGREDIENTS ·

· DIRECTIONS ·

_____

_____

_____

_____

_____

_____

_____

_____

_____

_____

_____

_____

_____

_____

About my Friend

How we met: _____

_____

How long we've known each other: _____

What's special about this recipe: _____

_____

A favorite memory with my friend: _____

_____

_____

My favorite thing about my friend: _____

_____

Recipe: _____

FROM THE KITCHEN OF: _____

· NOTES / TIPS ·

SERVINGS:

PREP / COOK TIME:

PREHEAT OVEN:

· INGREDIENTS ·

· DIRECTIONS ·

_____

_____

_____

_____

_____

_____

_____

_____

_____

_____

_____

_____

_____

_____

_____

About my Friend

How we met: _____

_____

How long we've known each other: _____

What's special about this recipe: _____

_____

A favorite memory with my friend: _____

_____

_____

My favorite thing about my friend: _____

_____

Recipe:

FROM THE KITCHEN OF:

SERVINGS:

PREP / COOK TIME:

PREHEAT OVEN:

· NOTES / TIPS ·

· INGREDIENTS ·

· DIRECTIONS ·

_____

_____

_____

_____

_____

_____

_____

_____

_____

_____

_____

_____

_____

_____

_____

About my Friend

How we met: _____

_____

How long we've known each other: _____

What's special about this recipe: _____

_____

A favorite memory with my friend: _____

_____

_____

My favorite thing about my friend: _____

_____

Recipe:

FROM THE KITCHEN OF: _____

SERVINGS:

PREP / COOK TIME:

PREHEAT OVEN:

· NOTES / TIPS ·

· INGREDIENTS ·

· DIRECTIONS ·

_____

_____

_____

_____

_____

_____

_____

_____

_____

_____

_____

_____

_____

_____

About my Friend

How we met: _____

_____

How long we've known each other: _____

What's special about this recipe: _____

_____

A favorite memory with my friend: _____

_____

_____

My favorite thing about my friend: _____

_____

· MORE NOTES ·

• SOUPS, SALADS, & SANDWICHES RECIPES •

1. Faceless Caesar Salad

2.

3.

4.

5.

6.

7.

8.

9.

10.

11.

12.

13.

14.

15.

16.

17.

18.

19.

20.

Recipe:

FROM THE KITCHEN OF: _____

SERVINGS:

PREP / COOK TIME:

PREHEAT OVEN:

· NOTES / TIPS ·

· INGREDIENTS ·

· DIRECTIONS ·

_____

_____

_____

_____

_____

_____

_____

_____

_____

_____

_____

_____

_____

_____

_____

About my Friend

How we met: _____

_____

How long we've known each other: _____

What's special about this recipe: _____

_____

A favorite memory with my friend: _____

_____

_____

My favorite thing about my friend: _____

_____

Recipe: _____

FROM THE KITCHEN OF: _____

· NOTES / TIPS ·

SERVINGS:

PREP / COOK TIME:

PREHEAT OVEN:

· INGREDIENTS ·

· DIRECTIONS ·

_____

_____

_____

_____

_____

_____

_____

_____

_____

_____

_____

_____

_____

_____

About my Friend

How we met: _____

_____

How long we've known each other: _____

What's special about this recipe: _____

_____

A favorite memory with my friend: _____

_____

_____

My favorite thing about my friend: _____

_____

Recipe: _____

FROM THE KITCHEN OF: _____

· NOTES / TIPS ·

SERVINGS:

PREP / COOK TIME:

PREHEAT OVEN:

_____
_____
_____
_____
_____
_____
_____
_____

· INGREDIENTS ·

_____ _____
_____ _____
_____ _____
_____ _____
_____ _____
_____ _____
_____ _____
_____ _____

· DIRECTIONS ·

_____

_____

_____

_____

_____

_____

_____

_____

_____

_____

_____

_____

About my Friend

How we met: _____

_____

How long we've known each other: _____

What's special about this recipe: _____

_____

A favorite memory with my friend: _____

_____

_____

My favorite thing about my friend: _____

_____

Recipe: _____

FROM THE KITCHEN OF: _____

SERVINGS:

PREP / COOK TIME:

PREHEAT OVEN:

· NOTES / TIPS ·

_____
_____
_____
_____
_____
_____
_____
_____

· INGREDIENTS ·

_____   _____
_____   _____
_____   _____
_____   _____
_____   _____
_____   _____
_____   _____
_____   _____
_____   _____

· DIRECTIONS ·

_____

_____

_____

_____

_____

_____

_____

_____

_____

_____

_____

_____

_____

About my Friend

How we met: _____

_____

How long we've known each other: _____

What's special about this recipe: _____

_____

A favorite memory with my friend: _____

_____

_____

My favorite thing about my friend: _____

_____

Recipe:

FROM THE KITCHEN OF:

SERVINGS:

PREP / COOK TIME:

PREHEAT OVEN:

· NOTES / TIPS ·

· INGREDIENTS ·

"That sandwich was the only good thing going on in my life!"

—Ross

· DIRECTIONS ·

_____
_____
_____
_____
_____
_____
_____
_____
_____
_____
_____
_____
_____

About my Friend

How we met: _____
_____

How long we've known each other: _____

What's special about this recipe: _____
_____

A favorite memory with my friend: _____
_____
_____

My favorite thing about my friend: _____
_____

Recipe: _____

FROM THE KITCHEN OF: _____

• NOTES / TIPS •

SERVINGS:

PREP / COOK TIME:

PREHEAT OVEN:

_____
_____
_____
_____
_____
_____
_____
_____

• INGREDIENTS •

_____   _____
_____   _____
_____   _____
_____   _____
_____   _____
_____   _____
_____   _____
_____   _____

· DIRECTIONS ·

_____

_____

_____

_____

_____

_____

_____

_____

_____

_____

_____

_____

_____

_____

About my Friend

How we met: _____

_____

How long we've known each other: _____

What's special about this recipe: _____

_____

A favorite memory with my friend: _____

_____

_____

My favorite thing about my friend: _____

_____

Recipe: _____

FROM THE KITCHEN OF: _____

SERVINGS:

PREP / COOK TIME:

PREHEAT OVEN:

• NOTES / TIPS •

_____
_____
_____
_____
_____
_____
_____
_____

• INGREDIENTS •

_____   _____
_____   _____
_____   _____
_____   _____
_____   _____
_____   _____
_____   _____
_____   _____
_____   _____

· DIRECTIONS ·

_____

_____

_____

_____

_____

_____

_____

_____

_____

_____

_____

_____

_____

_____

About my Friend

How we met: _____

_____

How long we've known each other: _____

What's special about this recipe: _____

_____

A favorite memory with my friend: _____

_____

_____

My favorite thing about my friend: _____

_____

Recipe: _____

FROM THE KITCHEN OF: _____

· NOTES / TIPS ·

SERVINGS: _____

PREP / COOK TIME: _____

PREHEAT OVEN: _____

· INGREDIENTS ·

· DIRECTIONS ·

_____

_____

_____

_____

_____

_____

_____

_____

_____

_____

_____

_____

_____

About my Friend

How we met: _____

_____

How long we've known each other: _____

What's special about this recipe: _____

_____

A favorite memory with my friend: _____

_____

_____

My favorite thing about my friend: _____

_____

Recipe:

FROM THE KITCHEN OF: _____

SERVINGS:

PREP / COOK TIME:

PREHEAT OVEN:

· NOTES / TIPS ·

_____
_____
_____
_____
_____
_____
_____
_____

· INGREDIENTS ·

_____ _____
_____ _____
_____ _____
_____ _____
_____ _____
_____ _____

· DIRECTIONS ·

_____
_____
_____
_____
_____
_____
_____
_____
_____
_____
_____
_____
_____
_____
_____
_____

About my Friend

How we met: _____
_____

How long we've known each other: _____

What's special about this recipe: _____
_____

A favorite memory with my friend: _____
_____
_____

My favorite thing about my friend: _____
_____

Recipe: _____

FROM THE KITCHEN OF: _____

· NOTES / TIPS ·

SERVINGS: _____

PREP / COOK TIME: _____

PREHEAT OVEN: _____

_____

_____

_____

· INGREDIENTS ·

_____   _____

_____   _____

_____   _____

_____   _____

_____   _____

_____   _____

_____   _____

"The fridge broke so I had to eat everything."

—Joey

· DIRECTIONS ·

_____
_____
_____
_____
_____
_____
_____
_____
_____
_____
_____
_____
_____

About my Friend

How we met: _____
_____

How long we've known each other: _____

What's special about this recipe: _____
_____

A favorite memory with my friend: _____
_____
_____

My favorite thing about my friend: _____
_____

Recipe: _____

FROM THE KITCHEN OF: _____

SERVINGS:

PREP / COOK TIME:

PREHEAT OVEN:

· NOTES / TIPS ·

_____
_____
_____
_____
_____
_____
_____
_____

· INGREDIENTS ·

_____ _____
_____ _____
_____ _____
_____ _____
_____ _____
_____ _____
_____ _____
_____ _____

· DIRECTIONS ·

_____

_____

_____

_____

_____

_____

_____

_____

_____

_____

_____

About my Friend

How we met: _____

_____

How long we've known each other: _____

What's special about this recipe: _____

_____

A favorite memory with my friend: _____

_____

_____

My favorite thing about my friend: _____

_____

Recipe: _____

FROM THE KITCHEN OF: _____

SERVINGS:

PREP / COOK TIME:

PREHEAT OVEN:

· NOTES / TIPS ·

· INGREDIENTS ·

· DIRECTIONS ·

_____

_____

_____

_____

_____

_____

_____

_____

_____

_____

_____

_____

_____

About my Friend

How we met: _____

_____

How long we've known each other: _____

What's special about this recipe: _____

_____

A favorite memory with my friend: _____

_____

_____

My favorite thing about my friend: _____

_____

Recipe:

FROM THE KITCHEN OF: _____

· NOTES / TIPS ·

SERVINGS:

PREP / COOK TIME:

PREHEAT OVEN:

· INGREDIENTS ·

· DIRECTIONS ·

_____

_____

_____

_____

_____

_____

_____

_____

_____

_____

_____

_____

_____

_____

_____

About my Friend

How we met: _____

_____

How long we've known each other: _____

What's special about this recipe: _____

_____

A favorite memory with my friend: _____

_____

_____

My favorite thing about my friend: _____

_____

Recipe: _____

FROM THE KITCHEN OF: _____

· NOTES / TIPS ·

SERVINGS:

PREP / COOK TIME:

PREHEAT OVEN:

_____
_____
_____
_____
_____
_____
_____
_____

· INGREDIENTS ·

_____ _____
_____ _____
_____ _____
_____ _____
_____ _____
_____ _____
_____ _____
_____ _____

· DIRECTIONS ·

_____
_____
_____
_____
_____
_____
_____
_____
_____
_____
_____
_____
_____
_____

About my Friend

How we met: _____
_____

How long we've known each other: _____

What's special about this recipe: _____
_____

A favorite memory with my friend: _____
_____
_____

My favorite thing about my friend: _____
_____

Recipe:

FROM THE KITCHEN OF:

· NOTES / TIPS ·

SERVINGS:

PREP / COOK TIME:

PREHEAT OVEN:

· INGREDIENTS ·

"I don't know. Why don't you just put it there next to my water."

—Rachel

· DIRECTIONS ·

_____

_____

_____

_____

_____

_____

_____

_____

_____

_____

_____

_____

_____

_____

_____

_____

About my Friend

How we met: _____

_____

How long we've known each other: _____

What's special about this recipe: _____

_____

A favorite memory with my friend: _____

_____

_____

My favorite thing about my friend: _____

_____

Recipe:

FROM THE KITCHEN OF: _____

SERVINGS:

PREP / COOK TIME:

PREHEAT OVEN:

• NOTES / TIPS •

• INGREDIENTS •

· DIRECTIONS ·

_____

_____

_____

_____

_____

_____

_____

_____

_____

_____

_____

_____

_____

_____

About my Friend

How we met: _____

_____

How long we've known each other: _____

What's special about this recipe: _____

_____

A favorite memory with my friend: _____

_____

_____

My favorite thing about my friend: _____

_____

Recipe: _____

FROM THE KITCHEN OF: _____

· NOTES / TIPS ·

SERVINGS:

PREP / COOK TIME:

PREHEAT OVEN:

_____
_____
_____
_____
_____
_____
_____
_____

· INGREDIENTS ·

_____ _____
_____ _____
_____ _____
_____ _____
_____ _____
_____ _____
_____ _____
_____ _____

· DIRECTIONS ·

_____
_____
_____
_____
_____
_____
_____
_____
_____
_____
_____
_____
_____
_____
_____

About my Friend

How we met: _____
_____

How long we've known each other: _____

What's special about this recipe: _____
_____

A favorite memory with my friend: _____
_____
_____

My favorite thing about my friend: _____
_____

Recipe: _____

FROM THE KITCHEN OF: _____

SERVINGS:

PREP / COOK TIME:

PREHEAT OVEN:

• NOTES / TIPS •

_____
_____
_____
_____
_____
_____
_____

• INGREDIENTS •

_____ _____
_____ _____
_____ _____
_____ _____
_____ _____
_____ _____
_____ _____

· DIRECTIONS ·

_____

_____

_____

_____

_____

_____

_____

_____

_____

_____

_____

_____

_____

About my Friend

How we met: _____

_____

How long we've known each other: _____

What's special about this recipe: _____

_____

A favorite memory with my friend: _____

_____

_____

My favorite thing about my friend: _____

_____

Recipe: _____

FROM THE KITCHEN OF: _____

· NOTES / TIPS ·

SERVINGS:

PREP / COOK TIME:

PREHEAT OVEN:

_____
_____
_____
_____
_____
_____
_____
_____

· INGREDIENTS ·

_____   _____
_____   _____
_____   _____
_____   _____
_____   _____
_____   _____
_____   _____
_____   _____

· DIRECTIONS ·

_____

_____

_____

_____

_____

_____

_____

_____

_____

_____

_____

_____

_____

About my Friend

How we met: _____

_____

How long we've known each other: _____

What's special about this recipe: _____

_____

A favorite memory with my friend: _____

_____

_____

My favorite thing about my friend: _____

_____

· MORE NOTES ·

· APPETIZERS RECIPES ·

1. Nacho Chair Nachos

2.

3.

4.

5.

6.

7.

8.

9.

10.

11.

12.

13.

14.

15.

16.

17.

18.

19.

20.

Recipe: _____

FROM THE KITCHEN OF: _____

SERVINGS:

PREP / COOK TIME:

PREHEAT OVEN:

· NOTES / TIPS ·

_____
_____
_____
_____
_____
_____
_____
_____

· INGREDIENTS ·

_____   _____
_____   _____
_____   _____
_____   _____
_____   _____
_____   _____
_____   _____
_____   _____

· DIRECTIONS ·

_____
_____
_____
_____
_____
_____
_____
_____
_____
_____
_____
_____
_____
_____

About my Friend

How we met: _____
_____

How long we've known each other: _____

What's special about this recipe: _____
_____

A favorite memory with my friend: _____
_____
_____

My favorite thing about my friend: _____
_____

Recipe: _____

FROM THE KITCHEN OF: _____

· NOTES / TIPS ·

_____
_____
_____
_____
_____
_____
_____
_____

SERVINGS:

PREP / COOK TIME:

PREHEAT OVEN:

· INGREDIENTS ·

_____   _____
_____   _____
_____   _____
_____   _____
_____   _____
_____   _____
_____   _____
_____   _____

· DIRECTIONS ·

_____

_____

_____

_____

_____

_____

_____

_____

_____

_____

_____

_____

_____

_____

About my Friend

How we met: _____

_____

How long we've known each other: _____

What's special about this recipe: _____

_____

A favorite memory with my friend: _____

_____

_____

My favorite thing about my friend: _____

_____

Recipe: _____

FROM THE KITCHEN OF: _____

· NOTES / TIPS ·

SERVINGS: _____

PREP / COOK TIME: _____

PREHEAT OVEN: _____

_____
_____
_____
_____
_____
_____
_____
_____

· INGREDIENTS ·

_____ _____
_____ _____
_____ _____
_____ _____
_____ _____
_____ _____
_____ _____
_____ _____

· DIRECTIONS ·

_____
_____
_____
_____
_____
_____
_____
_____
_____
_____
_____
_____
_____

About my Friend

How we met: _____
_____

How long we've known each other: _____

What's special about this recipe: _____
_____

A favorite memory with my friend: _____
_____
_____

My favorite thing about my friend: _____
_____

Recipe: _____

FROM THE KITCHEN OF: _____

· NOTES / TIPS ·

SERVINGS:

PREP / COOK TIME:

PREHEAT OVEN:

_____
_____
_____
_____
_____
_____
_____
_____

· INGREDIENTS ·

_____   _____
_____   _____
_____   _____
_____   _____
_____   _____
_____   _____
_____   _____
_____   _____

· DIRECTIONS ·

_____

_____

_____

_____

_____

_____

_____

_____

_____

_____

_____

_____

About my Friend

How we met: _____

_____

How long we've known each other: _____

What's special about this recipe: _____

_____

A favorite memory with my friend: _____

_____

_____

My favorite thing about my friend: _____

_____

Recipe: _____

FROM THE KITCHEN OF: _____

SERVINGS:

PREP / COOK TIME:

PREHEAT OVEN:

· NOTES / TIPS ·

_____
_____
_____
_____
_____
_____
_____
_____

· INGREDIENTS ·

_____   _____
_____   _____
_____   _____
_____   _____
_____   _____

"Cheese. It's milk... that you chew. Crackers.
Because your cheese needs a buddy."

—Chandler

· DIRECTIONS ·

_____

_____

_____

_____

_____

_____

_____

_____

_____

_____

_____

_____

_____

_____

About my Friend

How we met: _____

_____

How long we've known each other: _____

What's special about this recipe: _____

_____

A favorite memory with my friend: _____

_____

_____

My favorite thing about my friend: _____

_____

Recipe: _____

FROM THE KITCHEN OF: _____

SERVINGS:

PREP / COOK TIME:

PREHEAT OVEN:

· NOTES / TIPS ·

_____
_____
_____
_____
_____
_____
_____
_____

· INGREDIENTS ·

_____   _____
_____   _____
_____   _____
_____   _____
_____   _____
_____   _____
_____   _____
_____   _____

· DIRECTIONS ·

_____

_____

_____

_____

_____

_____

_____

_____

_____

_____

_____

_____

_____

_____

_____

_____

About my Friend

How we met: _____

_____

How long we've known each other: _____

What's special about this recipe: _____

_____

A favorite memory with my friend: _____

_____

_____

My favorite thing about my friend: _____

_____

Recipe: _____

FROM THE KITCHEN OF: _____

SERVINGS:

PREP / COOK TIME:

PREHEAT OVEN:

· NOTES / TIPS ·

_____
_____
_____
_____
_____
_____
_____
_____

· INGREDIENTS ·

_____   _____
_____   _____
_____   _____
_____   _____
_____   _____
_____   _____
_____   _____
_____   _____

· DIRECTIONS ·

_____

_____

_____

_____

_____

_____

_____

_____

_____

_____

_____

_____

_____

_____

_____

About my Friend

How we met: _____

_____

How long we've known each other: _____

What's special about this recipe: _____

_____

A favorite memory with my friend: _____

_____

_____

My favorite thing about my friend: _____

_____

Recipe: _____

FROM THE KITCHEN OF: _____

· NOTES / TIPS ·

SERVINGS:

PREP / COOK TIME:

PREHEAT OVEN:

_____
_____
_____
_____
_____
_____
_____
_____

· INGREDIENTS ·

_____   _____
_____   _____
_____   _____
_____   _____
_____   _____
_____   _____
_____   _____
_____   _____

· DIRECTIONS ·

_____

_____

_____

_____

_____

_____

_____

_____

_____

_____

_____

_____

About my Friend

How we met: _____

_____

How long we've known each other: _____

What's special about this recipe: _____

_____

A favorite memory with my friend: _____

_____

_____

My favorite thing about my friend: _____

_____

Recipe:

FROM THE KITCHEN OF: _____

SERVINGS:

PREP / COOK TIME:

PREHEAT OVEN:

· NOTES / TIPS ·

· INGREDIENTS ·

· DIRECTIONS ·

_____

_____

_____

_____

_____

_____

_____

_____

_____

_____

_____

_____

About my Friend

How we met: _____

_____

How long we've known each other: _____

What's special about this recipe: _____

_____

A favorite memory with my friend: _____

_____

_____

My favorite thing about my friend: _____

_____

Recipe:

FROM THE KITCHEN OF:

SERVINGS:

PREP / COOK TIME:

PREHEAT OVEN:

· NOTES / TIPS ·

· INGREDIENTS ·

"I don't know anything about cooking. I had to ask someone what it was called when the water makes those little bubbles."

—Monica

· DIRECTIONS ·

_____
_____
_____
_____
_____
_____
_____
_____
_____
_____
_____
_____
_____
_____

About my Friend

How we met: _____
_____

How long we've known each other: _____

What's special about this recipe: _____
_____

A favorite memory with my friend: _____
_____
_____

My favorite thing about my friend: _____
_____

Recipe:

FROM THE KITCHEN OF: _____

· NOTES / TIPS ·

SERVINGS:

PREP / COOK TIME:

PREHEAT OVEN:

· INGREDIENTS ·

· DIRECTIONS ·

_____
_____
_____
_____
_____
_____
_____
_____
_____
_____
_____
_____
_____

About my Friend

How we met: _____
_____

How long we've known each other: _____

What's special about this recipe: _____
_____

A favorite memory with my friend: _____
_____
_____

My favorite thing about my friend: _____
_____

Recipe: _____

FROM THE KITCHEN OF: _____

SERVINGS: _____

PREP / COOK TIME: _____

PREHEAT OVEN: _____

· NOTES / TIPS ·

_____

_____

_____

_____

_____

_____

_____

_____

· INGREDIENTS ·

_____   _____

_____   _____

_____   _____

_____   _____

_____   _____

_____   _____

_____   _____

_____   _____

_____   _____

· DIRECTIONS ·

_____

_____

_____

_____

_____

_____

_____

_____

_____

_____

_____

_____

_____

About my Friend

How we met: _____

_____

How long we've known each other: _____

What's special about this recipe: _____

_____

A favorite memory with my friend: _____

_____

_____

My favorite thing about my friend: _____

_____

Recipe:

FROM THE KITCHEN OF: _____

SERVINGS:

PREP / COOK TIME:

PREHEAT OVEN:

· NOTES / TIPS ·

· INGREDIENTS ·

· DIRECTIONS ·

_____

_____

_____

_____

_____

_____

_____

_____

_____

_____

_____

_____

_____

_____

_____

About my Friend

How we met: _____

_____

How long we've known each other: _____

What's special about this recipe: _____

_____

A favorite memory with my friend: _____

_____

_____

My favorite thing about my friend: _____

_____

Recipe: _____

FROM THE KITCHEN OF: _____

• NOTES / TIPS •

SERVINGS:

PREP / COOK TIME:

PREHEAT OVEN:

_____
_____
_____
_____
_____
_____
_____

• INGREDIENTS •

_____   _____
_____   _____
_____   _____
_____   _____
_____   _____
_____   _____
_____   _____
_____   _____

· DIRECTIONS ·

_____

_____

_____

_____

_____

_____

_____

_____

_____

_____

_____

_____

_____

About my Friend

How we met: _____

_____

How long we've known each other: _____

What's special about this recipe: _____

_____

A favorite memory with my friend: _____

_____

_____

My favorite thing about my friend: _____

_____

Recipe:

FROM THE KITCHEN OF:

SERVINGS:

PREP / COOK TIME:

PREHEAT OVEN:

· NOTES / TIPS ·

· INGREDIENTS ·

"No girl—no matter how hot—can be forgiven for stealing French fries from his plate."

—Joey

· DIRECTIONS ·

_____
_____
_____
_____
_____
_____
_____
_____
_____
_____
_____
_____
_____

About my Friend

How we met: _____
_____

How long we've known each other: _____

What's special about this recipe: _____
_____

A favorite memory with my friend: _____
_____
_____

My favorite thing about my friend: _____
_____

Recipe:

FROM THE KITCHEN OF: _____

· NOTES / TIPS ·

SERVINGS:

PREP / COOK TIME:

PREHEAT OVEN:

· INGREDIENTS ·

· DIRECTIONS ·

_____

_____

_____

_____

_____

_____

_____

_____

_____

_____

_____

_____

_____

About my Friend

How we met: _____

_____

How long we've known each other: _____

What's special about this recipe: _____

_____

A favorite memory with my friend: _____

_____

_____

My favorite thing about my friend: _____

_____

Recipe:

FROM THE KITCHEN OF: _____

SERVINGS:

PREP / COOK TIME:

PREHEAT OVEN:

· NOTES / TIPS ·

· INGREDIENTS ·

· DIRECTIONS ·

_____

_____

_____

_____

_____

_____

_____

_____

_____

_____

_____

_____

About my Friend

How we met: _____

_____

How long we've known each other: _____

What's special about this recipe: _____

_____

A favorite memory with my friend: _____

_____

_____

My favorite thing about my friend: _____

_____

Recipe: _____

FROM THE KITCHEN OF: _____

SERVINGS:

PREP / COOK TIME:

PREHEAT OVEN:

· NOTES / TIPS ·

· INGREDIENTS ·

· DIRECTIONS ·

_____
_____
_____
_____
_____
_____
_____
_____
_____
_____
_____
_____
_____
_____

About my Friend

How we met: _____
_____

How long we've known each other: _____

What's special about this recipe: _____
_____

A favorite memory with my friend: _____
_____
_____

My favorite thing about my friend: _____
_____

Recipe:

FROM THE KITCHEN OF: _____

· NOTES / TIPS ·

SERVINGS:

PREP / COOK TIME:

PREHEAT OVEN:

· INGREDIENTS ·

· DIRECTIONS ·

_____

_____

_____

_____

_____

_____

_____

_____

_____

_____

_____

_____

About my Friend

How we met: _____

_____

How long we've known each other: _____

What's special about this recipe: _____

_____

A favorite memory with my friend: _____

_____

_____

My favorite thing about my friend: _____

_____

· MORE NOTES ·

Sides

AND Starters

1950s
Diner Fries

2 russet potatoes, about 1½ pounds total, scrubbed and quartered
2 tablespoons olive oil
Kosher salt and freshly ground pepper
3 tablespoons malt vinegar, plus more for serving
Ketchup or aioli, for serving

Cut each potato quarter into 5 wedges. Pile the potatoes on a baking sheet lined with parchment paper. Drizzle with the olive oil, season well with salt and pepper, and toss to coat. Spread the potatoes in a single layer and roast in the upper third of the oven, turning once about halfway through, until golden brown on the edges and fork-tender, about 25 minutes. While the fries are still hot, carefully transfer them to a bowl. Immediately sprinkle with the vinegar and more salt. Let sit for a few minutes, then serve with ketchup or aioli.

"Hey, how'd the interview go?" —Rachel

"It bit. It was a '50s theme restaurant. I'd have to cook in a costume and dance on the counter. I mean, I was a sous chef at Cafe des Artistes. How can I take a job where I have to make something called Laverne-and-Curly Fries?" —Monica

• SIDES & STARTERS RECIPES •

1. 1950s Diner Fries

2.

3.

4.

5.

6.

7.

8.

9.

10.

11.

12.

13.

14.

15.

16.

17.

18.

19.

20.

Recipe:

FROM THE KITCHEN OF: _____

SERVINGS:

PREP / COOK TIME:

PREHEAT OVEN:

• NOTES / TIPS •

• INGREDIENTS •

· DIRECTIONS ·

_____

_____

_____

_____

_____

_____

_____

_____

_____

_____

_____

_____

About my Friend

How we met: _____

_____

How long we've known each other: _____

What's special about this recipe: _____

_____

A favorite memory with my friend: _____

_____

_____

My favorite thing about my friend: _____

_____

Recipe: _____

FROM THE KITCHEN OF: _____

SERVINGS:

PREP / COOK TIME:

PREHEAT OVEN:

· NOTES / TIPS ·

_____
_____
_____
_____
_____
_____
_____

· INGREDIENTS ·

_____   _____
_____   _____
_____   _____
_____   _____
_____   _____
_____   _____
_____   _____
_____   _____

· DIRECTIONS ·

_____

_____

_____

_____

_____

_____

_____

_____

_____

_____

_____

_____

_____

_____

_____

About my Friend

How we met: _____

_____

How long we've known each other: _____

What's special about this recipe: _____

_____

A favorite memory with my friend: _____

_____

_____

My favorite thing about my friend: _____

_____

Recipe: _____

FROM THE KITCHEN OF: _____

SERVINGS:

PREP / COOK TIME:

PREHEAT OVEN:

· NOTES / TIPS ·

_____
_____
_____
_____
_____
_____
_____
_____

· INGREDIENTS ·

_____   _____
_____   _____
_____   _____
_____   _____
_____   _____
_____   _____
_____   _____
_____   _____

· DIRECTIONS ·

_____
_____
_____
_____
_____
_____
_____
_____
_____
_____
_____
_____
_____
_____
_____

About my Friend

How we met: _____
_____

How long we've known each other: _____

What's special about this recipe: _____
_____

A favorite memory with my friend: _____
_____
_____

My favorite thing about my friend: _____
_____

Recipe:

FROM THE KITCHEN OF: _____

SERVINGS:

PREP / COOK TIME:

PREHEAT OVEN:

· NOTES / TIPS ·

· INGREDIENTS ·

· DIRECTIONS ·

_____

_____

_____

_____

_____

_____

_____

_____

_____

_____

_____

_____

About my Friend

How we met: _____

_____

How long we've known each other: _____

What's special about this recipe: _____

_____

A favorite memory with my friend: _____

_____

_____

My favorite thing about my friend: _____

_____

Recipe:

FROM THE KITCHEN OF:

SERVINGS:

PREP / COOK TIME:

PREHEAT OVEN:

· NOTES / TIPS ·

· INGREDIENTS ·

"Oh my god it's brussels sprouts!" —Rachel

"That's worse than no food!" —Ross

· DIRECTIONS ·

_____

_____

_____

_____

_____

_____

_____

_____

_____

_____

_____

_____

_____

_____

About my Friend

How we met: _____

_____

How long we've known each other: _____

What's special about this recipe: _____

_____

A favorite memory with my friend: _____

_____

_____

My favorite thing about my friend: _____

_____

Recipe: _____

FROM THE KITCHEN OF: _____

SERVINGS:

PREP / COOK TIME:

PREHEAT OVEN:

· NOTES / TIPS ·

_____
_____
_____
_____
_____
_____
_____

· INGREDIENTS ·

_____ _____
_____ _____
_____ _____
_____ _____
_____ _____
_____ _____
_____ _____

· DIRECTIONS ·

_____

_____

_____

_____

_____

_____

_____

_____

_____

_____

_____

_____

_____

_____

About my Friend

How we met: _____

_____

How long we've known each other: _____

What's special about this recipe: _____

_____

A favorite memory with my friend: _____

_____

_____

My favorite thing about my friend: _____

_____

Recipe:

FROM THE KITCHEN OF: _____

· NOTES / TIPS ·

SERVINGS:

PREP / COOK TIME:

PREHEAT OVEN:

· INGREDIENTS ·

· DIRECTIONS ·

_____

_____

_____

_____

_____

_____

_____

_____

_____

_____

_____

_____

_____

About my Friend

How we met: _____

_____

How long we've known each other: _____

What's special about this recipe: _____

_____

A favorite memory with my friend: _____

_____

_____

My favorite thing about my friend: _____

_____

Recipe:

FROM THE KITCHEN OF: _____

· NOTES / TIPS ·

SERVINGS:

PREP / COOK TIME:

PREHEAT OVEN:

· INGREDIENTS ·

· DIRECTIONS ·

_____

_____

_____

_____

_____

_____

_____

_____

_____

_____

_____

_____

_____

About my Friend

How we met: _____

_____

How long we've known each other: _____

What's special about this recipe: _____

_____

A favorite memory with my friend: _____

_____

_____

My favorite thing about my friend: _____

_____

Recipe:

FROM THE KITCHEN OF: _____

· NOTES / TIPS ·

SERVINGS:

PREP / COOK TIME:

PREHEAT OVEN:

· INGREDIENTS ·

· DIRECTIONS ·

_____
_____
_____
_____
_____
_____
_____
_____
_____
_____
_____
_____
_____
_____

About my Friend

How we met: _____
_____

How long we've known each other: _____

What's special about this recipe: _____
_____

A favorite memory with my friend: _____
_____
_____

My favorite thing about my friend: _____
_____

Recipe:

FROM THE KITCHEN OF:

· NOTES / TIPS ·

SERVINGS:

PREP / COOK TIME:

PREHEAT OVEN:

· INGREDIENTS ·

"Once, Monica was sent to her room without dinner, so she ate the macaroni off a jewelry box she'd made."

—Ross

· DIRECTIONS ·

_____
_____
_____
_____
_____
_____
_____
_____
_____
_____
_____
_____

About my Friend

How we met: _____
_____

How long we've known each other: _____

What's special about this recipe: _____
_____

A favorite memory with my friend: _____
_____
_____

My favorite thing about my friend: _____
_____

Recipe:

FROM THE KITCHEN OF: _____

· NOTES / TIPS ·

SERVINGS:

PREP / COOK TIME:

PREHEAT OVEN:

· INGREDIENTS ·

· DIRECTIONS ·

_____
_____
_____
_____
_____
_____
_____
_____
_____
_____
_____
_____
_____
_____

About my Friend

How we met: _____
_____

How long we've known each other: _____

What's special about this recipe: _____
_____

A favorite memory with my friend: _____
_____
_____

My favorite thing about my friend: _____

Recipe: _____

FROM THE KITCHEN OF: _____

SERVINGS:

PREP / COOK TIME:

PREHEAT OVEN:

· NOTES / TIPS ·

_____
_____
_____
_____
_____
_____
_____
_____

· INGREDIENTS ·

_____   _____
_____   _____
_____   _____
_____   _____
_____   _____
_____   _____
_____   _____
_____   _____

· DIRECTIONS ·

_____

_____

_____

_____

_____

_____

_____

_____

_____

_____

_____

_____

_____

_____

_____

About my Friend

How we met: _____

_____

How long we've known each other: _____

What's special about this recipe: _____

_____

A favorite memory with my friend: _____

_____

_____

My favorite thing about my friend: _____

_____

Recipe: _____

FROM THE KITCHEN OF: _____

· NOTES / TIPS ·

SERVINGS:

PREP / COOK TIME:

PREHEAT OVEN:

· INGREDIENTS ·

· DIRECTIONS ·

_____

_____

_____

_____

_____

_____

_____

_____

_____

_____

_____

_____

_____

_____

About my Friend

How we met: _____

_____

How long we've known each other: _____

What's special about this recipe: _____

_____

A favorite memory with my friend: _____

_____

_____

My favorite thing about my friend: _____

_____

Recipe: _____

FROM THE KITCHEN OF: _____

· NOTES / TIPS ·

SERVINGS:

PREP / COOK TIME:

PREHEAT OVEN:

· INGREDIENTS ·

· DIRECTIONS ·

_____

_____

_____

_____

_____

_____

_____

_____

_____

_____

_____

_____

_____

About my Friend

How we met: _____

_____

How long we've known each other: _____

What's special about this recipe: _____

_____

A favorite memory with my friend: _____

_____

_____

My favorite thing about my friend: _____

_____

Recipe:

FROM THE KITCHEN OF:

SERVINGS:

PREP / COOK TIME:

PREHEAT OVEN:

• NOTES / TIPS •

• INGREDIENTS •

"That's a great story. Can I eat it?"

—Joey

· DIRECTIONS ·

_____
_____
_____
_____
_____
_____
_____
_____
_____
_____
_____
_____
_____
_____

About my Friend

How we met: _____
_____

How long we've known each other: _____

What's special about this recipe: _____
_____

A favorite memory with my friend: _____
_____
_____

My favorite thing about my friend: _____
_____

Recipe: _____

FROM THE KITCHEN OF: _____

· NOTES / TIPS ·

SERVINGS:

PREP / COOK TIME:

PREHEAT OVEN:

_____
_____
_____
_____
_____
_____
_____
_____

· INGREDIENTS ·

_____   _____
_____   _____
_____   _____
_____   _____
_____   _____
_____   _____
_____   _____
_____   _____

· DIRECTIONS ·

_____
_____
_____
_____
_____
_____
_____
_____
_____
_____
_____
_____
_____

About my Friend

How we met: _____
_____

How long we've known each other: _____

What's special about this recipe: _____
_____

A favorite memory with my friend: _____
_____
_____

My favorite thing about my friend: _____
_____

Recipe:

FROM THE KITCHEN OF: _____

SERVINGS:

PREP / COOK TIME:

PREHEAT OVEN:

· NOTES / TIPS ·

· INGREDIENTS ·

· DIRECTIONS ·

_____

_____

_____

_____

_____

_____

_____

_____

_____

_____

_____

_____

_____

_____

_____

_____

About my Friend

How we met: _____

_____

How long we've known each other: _____

What's special about this recipe: _____

_____

A favorite memory with my friend: _____

_____

_____

My favorite thing about my friend: _____

_____

Recipe:

FROM THE KITCHEN OF: _____

SERVINGS:

PREP / COOK TIME:

PREHEAT OVEN:

· NOTES / TIPS ·

· INGREDIENTS ·

· DIRECTIONS ·

_____

_____

_____

_____

_____

_____

_____

_____

_____

_____

_____

_____

_____

_____

About my Friend

How we met: _____

_____

How long we've known each other: _____

What's special about this recipe: _____

_____

A favorite memory with my friend: _____

_____

_____

My favorite thing about my friend: _____

_____

Recipe:

FROM THE KITCHEN OF: _____

SERVINGS:

PREP / COOK TIME:

PREHEAT OVEN:

· NOTES / TIPS ·

· INGREDIENTS ·

· DIRECTIONS ·

_____

_____

_____

_____

_____

_____

_____

_____

_____

_____

_____

_____

About my Friend

How we met: _____

_____

How long we've known each other: _____

What's special about this recipe: _____

_____

A favorite memory with my friend: _____

_____

_____

My favorite thing about my friend: _____

_____

· MORE NOTES ·

· MAINS RECIPES ·

1. Monica's Innocent Burger

2.

3.

4.

5.

6.

7.

8.

9.

10.

11.

12.

13.

14.

15.

16.

17.

18.

19.

20.

Recipe: _____

FROM THE KITCHEN OF: _____

· NOTES / TIPS ·

SERVINGS:

PREP / COOK TIME:

PREHEAT OVEN:

_____
_____
_____
_____
_____
_____
_____
_____

· INGREDIENTS ·

_____ _____
_____ _____
_____ _____
_____ _____
_____ _____
_____ _____
_____ _____
_____ _____

· DIRECTIONS ·

_____

_____

_____

_____

_____

_____

_____

_____

_____

_____

_____

_____

_____

_____

About my Friend

How we met: _____

_____

How long we've known each other: _____

What's special about this recipe: _____

_____

A favorite memory with my friend: _____

_____

_____

My favorite thing about my friend: _____

_____

Recipe: _____

FROM THE KITCHEN OF: _____

· NOTES / TIPS ·

SERVINGS:

PREP / COOK TIME:

PREHEAT OVEN:

_____
_____
_____
_____
_____
_____
_____
_____

· INGREDIENTS ·

_____ _____
_____ _____
_____ _____
_____ _____
_____ _____
_____ _____
_____ _____
_____ _____

· DIRECTIONS ·

_____

_____

_____

_____

_____

_____

_____

_____

_____

_____

_____

_____

_____

_____

_____

About my Friend

How we met: _____

_____

How long we've known each other: _____

What's special about this recipe: _____

_____

A favorite memory with my friend: _____

_____

_____

My favorite thing about my friend: _____

_____

Recipe: _____

FROM THE KITCHEN OF: _____

· NOTES / TIPS ·

_____
_____
_____
_____
_____
_____
_____
_____

SERVINGS:

PREP / COOK TIME:

PREHEAT OVEN:

· INGREDIENTS ·

_____   _____
_____   _____
_____   _____
_____   _____
_____   _____
_____   _____
_____   _____
_____   _____

· DIRECTIONS ·

_____

_____

_____

_____

_____

_____

_____

_____

_____

_____

_____

_____

_____

_____

About my Friend

How we met: _____

_____

How long we've known each other: _____

What's special about this recipe: _____

_____

A favorite memory with my friend: _____

_____

_____

My favorite thing about my friend: _____

_____

Recipe: _____

FROM THE KITCHEN OF: _____

SERVINGS:

PREP / COOK TIME:

PREHEAT OVEN:

· NOTES / TIPS ·

_____
_____
_____
_____
_____
_____
_____

· INGREDIENTS ·

_____ _____
_____ _____
_____ _____
_____ _____
_____ _____
_____ _____
_____ _____
_____ _____

· DIRECTIONS ·

_____

_____

_____

_____

_____

_____

_____

_____

_____

_____

_____

_____

_____

_____

About my Friend

How we met: _____

_____

How long we've known each other: _____

What's special about this recipe: _____

_____

A favorite memory with my friend: _____

_____

_____

My favorite thing about my friend: _____

_____

Recipe: _____

FROM THE KITCHEN OF: _____

SERVINGS:

PREP / COOK TIME:

PREHEAT OVEN:

· NOTES / TIPS ·

_____
_____
_____
_____
_____
_____
_____

· INGREDIENTS ·

_____ _____
_____ _____
_____ _____
_____ _____
_____ _____

"Don't you put words in people's mouths.
You put turkey in people's mouths."

—Joey

· DIRECTIONS ·

_____

_____

_____

_____

_____

_____

_____

_____

_____

_____

_____

_____

About my Friend

How we met: _____

_____

How long we've known each other: _____

What's special about this recipe: _____

_____

A favorite memory with my friend: _____

_____

_____

My favorite thing about my friend: _____

_____

Recipe: _____

FROM THE KITCHEN OF: _____

· NOTES / TIPS ·

SERVINGS:

PREP / COOK TIME:

PREHEAT OVEN:

_____
_____
_____
_____
_____
_____
_____
_____

· INGREDIENTS ·

_____   _____
_____   _____
_____   _____
_____   _____
_____   _____
_____   _____
_____   _____
_____   _____
_____   _____

· DIRECTIONS ·

_____

_____

_____

_____

_____

_____

_____

_____

_____

_____

_____

_____

About my Friend

How we met: _____

_____

How long we've known each other: _____

What's special about this recipe: _____

_____

A favorite memory with my friend: _____

_____

_____

My favorite thing about my friend: _____

_____

Recipe: _____

FROM THE KITCHEN OF: _____

• NOTES / TIPS •

SERVINGS:

PREP / COOK TIME:

PREHEAT OVEN:

• INGREDIENTS •

· DIRECTIONS ·

_____

_____

_____

_____

_____

_____

_____

_____

_____

_____

_____

_____

_____

_____

About my Friend

How we met: _____

_____

How long we've known each other: _____

What's special about this recipe: _____

_____

A favorite memory with my friend: _____

_____

_____

My favorite thing about my friend: _____

_____

Recipe: _____

FROM THE KITCHEN OF: _____

SERVINGS:

PREP / COOK TIME:

PREHEAT OVEN:

· NOTES / TIPS ·

_____
_____
_____
_____
_____
_____
_____
_____

· INGREDIENTS ·

_____   _____
_____   _____
_____   _____
_____   _____
_____   _____
_____   _____
_____   _____
_____   _____
_____   _____

· DIRECTIONS ·

_____

_____

_____

_____

_____

_____

_____

_____

_____

_____

_____

_____

_____

About my Friend

How we met: _____

_____

How long we've known each other: _____

What's special about this recipe: _____

_____

A favorite memory with my friend: _____

_____

_____

My favorite thing about my friend: _____

_____

Recipe:

FROM THE KITCHEN OF: _____

· NOTES / TIPS ·

SERVINGS:

PREP / COOK TIME:

PREHEAT OVEN:

· INGREDIENTS ·

· DIRECTIONS ·

_____

_____

_____

_____

_____

_____

_____

_____

_____

_____

_____

_____

About my Friend

How we met: _____

_____

How long we've known each other: _____

What's special about this recipe: _____

_____

A favorite memory with my friend: _____

_____

_____

My favorite thing about my friend: _____

_____

Recipe:

FROM THE KITCHEN OF:

· NOTES / TIPS ·

SERVINGS:

PREP / COOK TIME:

PREHEAT OVEN:

· INGREDIENTS ·

"Unagi is a state of total awareness. OK? Only by achieving true unagi can you be prepared for any danger that may befall you."

—Ross

· DIRECTIONS ·

_____
_____
_____
_____
_____
_____
_____
_____
_____
_____
_____
_____
_____

About my Friend

How we met: _____
_____

How long we've known each other: _____

What's special about this recipe: _____
_____

A favorite memory with my friend: _____
_____
_____

My favorite thing about my friend: _____
_____

Recipe:

FROM THE KITCHEN OF: _____

SERVINGS:

PREP / COOK TIME:

PREHEAT OVEN:

· NOTES / TIPS ·

· INGREDIENTS ·

· DIRECTIONS ·

_____

_____

_____

_____

_____

_____

_____

_____

_____

_____

_____

_____

About my Friend

How we met: _____

_____

How long we've known each other: _____

What's special about this recipe: _____

_____

A favorite memory with my friend: _____

_____

_____

My favorite thing about my friend: _____

_____

Recipe: _____

FROM THE KITCHEN OF: _____

SERVINGS:

PREP / COOK TIME:

PREHEAT OVEN:

· NOTES / TIPS ·

_____
_____
_____
_____
_____
_____
_____
_____

· INGREDIENTS ·

_____   _____
_____   _____
_____   _____
_____   _____
_____   _____
_____   _____
_____   _____

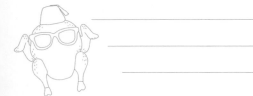

· DIRECTIONS ·

_____

_____

_____

_____

_____

_____

_____

_____

_____

_____

_____

_____

_____

_____

About my Friend

How we met: _____

_____

How long we've known each other: _____

What's special about this recipe: _____

_____

A favorite memory with my friend: _____

_____

_____

My favorite thing about my friend: _____

_____

Recipe:

FROM THE KITCHEN OF: _____

· NOTES / TIPS ·

SERVINGS:

PREP / COOK TIME:

PREHEAT OVEN:

· INGREDIENTS ·

· DIRECTIONS ·

_____
_____
_____
_____
_____
_____
_____
_____
_____
_____
_____
_____
_____

About my Friend

How we met: _____

_____

How long we've known each other: _____

What's special about this recipe: _____

_____

A favorite memory with my friend: _____

_____

_____

My favorite thing about my friend: _____

_____

Recipe: _____

FROM THE KITCHEN OF: _____

SERVINGS:

PREP / COOK TIME:

PREHEAT OVEN:

· NOTES / TIPS ·

· INGREDIENTS ·

· DIRECTIONS ·

_____
_____
_____
_____
_____
_____
_____
_____
_____
_____
_____
_____
_____
_____
_____

About my Friend

How we met: _____
_____

How long we've known each other: _____
What's special about this recipe: _____
_____

A favorite memory with my friend: _____
_____
_____

My favorite thing about my friend: _____
_____

Recipe:

FROM THE KITCHEN OF:

SERVINGS:

PREP / COOK TIME:

PREHEAT OVEN:

· NOTES / TIPS ·

· INGREDIENTS ·

"Here come the meat sweats."

—Ross

· DIRECTIONS ·

_____

_____

_____

_____

_____

_____

_____

_____

_____

_____

_____

_____

_____

About my Friend

How we met: _____

_____

How long we've known each other: _____

What's special about this recipe: _____

_____

A favorite memory with my friend: _____

_____

_____

My favorite thing about my friend: _____

_____

Recipe: _____

FROM THE KITCHEN OF: _____

SERVINGS:

PREP / COOK TIME:

PREHEAT OVEN:

· NOTES / TIPS ·

_____
_____
_____
_____
_____
_____
_____

· INGREDIENTS ·

_____   _____
_____   _____
_____   _____
_____   _____
_____   _____
_____   _____
_____   _____
_____   _____
_____   _____

· DIRECTIONS ·

_____

_____

_____

_____

_____

_____

_____

_____

_____

_____

_____

_____

_____

About my Friend

How we met: _____

_____

How long we've known each other: _____

What's special about this recipe: _____

_____

A favorite memory with my friend: _____

_____

_____

My favorite thing about my friend: _____

_____

Recipe: _____

FROM THE KITCHEN OF: _____

SERVINGS:

PREP / COOK TIME:

PREHEAT OVEN:

· NOTES / TIPS ·

_____
_____
_____
_____
_____
_____
_____
_____

· INGREDIENTS ·

_____   _____
_____   _____
_____   _____
_____   _____
_____   _____
_____   _____
_____   _____

· DIRECTIONS ·

_____

_____

_____

_____

_____

_____

_____

_____

_____

_____

_____

_____

_____

About my Friend

How we met: _____

_____

How long we've known each other: _____

What's special about this recipe: _____

_____

A favorite memory with my friend: _____

_____

_____

My favorite thing about my friend: _____

_____

Recipe:

FROM THE KITCHEN OF: _____

SERVINGS:

PREP / COOK TIME:

PREHEAT OVEN:

· NOTES / TIPS ·

· INGREDIENTS ·

· DIRECTIONS ·

_____

_____

_____

_____

_____

_____

_____

_____

_____

_____

_____

_____

_____

About my Friend

How we met: _____

_____

How long we've known each other: _____

What's special about this recipe: _____

_____

A favorite memory with my friend: _____

_____

_____

My favorite thing about my friend: _____

_____

Recipe: _____

FROM THE KITCHEN OF: _____

• NOTES / TIPS •

SERVINGS:

PREP / COOK TIME:

PREHEAT OVEN:

• INGREDIENTS •

· DIRECTIONS ·

_____

_____

_____

_____

_____

_____

_____

_____

_____

_____

_____

_____

_____

About my Friend

How we met: _____

_____

How long we've known each other: _____

What's special about this recipe: _____

_____

A favorite memory with my friend: _____

_____

_____

My favorite thing about my friend: _____

_____

· DESSERTS & DRINKS RECIPES ·

1. Cheesecake Worth Stealing

2.

3.

4.

5.

6.

7.

8.

9.

10.

11.

12.

13.

14.

15.

16.

17.

18.

19.

20.

Recipe:

FROM THE KITCHEN OF: _____

· NOTES / TIPS ·

SERVINGS:

PREP / COOK TIME:

PREHEAT OVEN:

· INGREDIENTS ·

· DIRECTIONS ·

_____

_____

_____

_____

_____

_____

_____

_____

_____

_____

_____

_____

_____

_____

About my Friend

How we met: _____

_____

How long we've known each other: _____

What's special about this recipe: _____

_____

A favorite memory with my friend: _____

_____

_____

My favorite thing about my friend: _____

_____

Recipe:

FROM THE KITCHEN OF:

SERVINGS:

PREP / COOK TIME:

PREHEAT OVEN:

· NOTES / TIPS ·

· INGREDIENTS ·

· DIRECTIONS ·

_____

_____

_____

_____

_____

_____

_____

_____

_____

_____

_____

_____

_____

About my Friend

How we met: _____

_____

How long we've known each other: _____

What's special about this recipe: _____

_____

A favorite memory with my friend: _____

_____

_____

My favorite thing about my friend: _____

_____

Recipe:

FROM THE KITCHEN OF: _____

· NOTES / TIPS ·

SERVINGS:

PREP / COOK TIME:

PREHEAT OVEN:

· INGREDIENTS ·

· DIRECTIONS ·

_____
_____
_____
_____
_____
_____
_____
_____
_____
_____
_____
_____
_____

About my Friend

How we met: _____
_____

How long we've known each other: _____

What's special about this recipe: _____
_____

A favorite memory with my friend: _____
_____
_____

My favorite thing about my friend: _____
_____

Recipe: _____

FROM THE KITCHEN OF: _____

· NOTES / TIPS ·

SERVINGS:

PREP / COOK TIME:

PREHEAT OVEN:

· INGREDIENTS ·

· DIRECTIONS ·

_____

_____

_____

_____

_____

_____

_____

_____

_____

_____

_____

_____

_____

_____

About my Friend

How we met: _____

_____

How long we've known each other: _____

What's special about this recipe: _____

_____

A favorite memory with my friend: _____

_____

_____

My favorite thing about my friend: _____

_____

Recipe:

FROM THE KITCHEN OF:

· NOTES / TIPS ·

SERVINGS:

PREP / COOK TIME:

PREHEAT OVEN:

· INGREDIENTS ·

"No matter what happens... We still get cake right?"

—Joey

· DIRECTIONS ·

_____

_____

_____

_____

_____

_____

_____

_____

_____

_____

_____

_____

_____

_____

_____

About my Friend

How we met: _____

_____

How long we've known each other: _____

What's special about this recipe: _____

_____

A favorite memory with my friend: _____

_____

_____

My favorite thing about my friend: _____

_____

Recipe: _____

FROM THE KITCHEN OF: _____

· NOTES / TIPS ·

SERVINGS:

PREP / COOK TIME:

PREHEAT OVEN:

_____
_____
_____
_____
_____
_____
_____

· INGREDIENTS ·

_____ _____
_____ _____
_____ _____
_____ _____
_____ _____
_____ _____
_____ _____
_____ _____

· DIRECTIONS ·

_____
_____
_____
_____
_____
_____
_____
_____
_____
_____
_____
_____
_____

About my Friend

How we met: _____
_____

How long we've known each other: _____

What's special about this recipe: _____
_____

A favorite memory with my friend: _____
_____
_____

My favorite thing about my friend: _____
_____

Recipe: _____

FROM THE KITCHEN OF: _____

· NOTES / TIPS ·

SERVINGS:

PREP / COOK TIME:

PREHEAT OVEN:

· INGREDIENTS ·

· DIRECTIONS ·

_____
_____
_____
_____
_____
_____
_____
_____
_____
_____
_____
_____

About my Friend

How we met: _____
_____

How long we've known each other: _____

What's special about this recipe: _____
_____

A favorite memory with my friend: _____
_____
_____

My favorite thing about my friend: _____
_____

Recipe: _____

FROM THE KITCHEN OF: _____

· NOTES / TIPS ·

SERVINGS:

PREP / COOK TIME:

PREHEAT OVEN:

· INGREDIENTS ·

· DIRECTIONS ·

_____

_____

_____

_____

_____

_____

_____

_____

_____

_____

_____

_____

_____

_____

About my Friend

How we met: _____

_____

How long we've known each other: _____

What's special about this recipe: _____

_____

A favorite memory with my friend: _____

_____

_____

My favorite thing about my friend: _____

_____

Recipe: _____

FROM THE KITCHEN OF: _____

· NOTES / TIPS ·

SERVINGS:

PREP / COOK TIME:

PREHEAT OVEN:

_____
_____
_____
_____
_____
_____
_____

· INGREDIENTS ·

· DIRECTIONS ·

_____
_____
_____
_____
_____
_____
_____
_____
_____
_____
_____
_____
_____
_____
_____
_____

About my Friend

How we met: _____
_____

How long we've known each other: _____

What's special about this recipe: _____
_____

A favorite memory with my friend: _____
_____
_____

My favorite thing about my friend: _____
_____

Recipe: _____

FROM THE KITCHEN OF: _____

· NOTES / TIPS ·

SERVINGS: _____

PREP / COOK TIME: _____

PREHEAT OVEN: _____

· INGREDIENTS ·

_____ _____

_____ _____

_____ _____

_____ _____

_____ _____

_____ _____

"I'm full, and yet I know if I stop eating this, I'll regret it."

—Chandler

· DIRECTIONS ·

_____

_____

_____

_____

_____

_____

_____

_____

_____

_____

_____

_____

_____

About my Friend

How we met: _____

_____

How long we've known each other: _____

What's special about this recipe: _____

_____

A favorite memory with my friend: _____

_____

_____

My favorite thing about my friend: _____

_____

Recipe:

FROM THE KITCHEN OF:

SERVINGS:

PREP / COOK TIME:

PREHEAT OVEN:

· NOTES / TIPS ·

· INGREDIENTS ·

· DIRECTIONS ·

_____

_____

_____

_____

_____

_____

_____

_____

_____

_____

_____

_____

_____

_____

About my Friend

How we met: _____

_____

How long we've known each other: _____

What's special about this recipe: _____

_____

A favorite memory with my friend: _____

_____

_____

My favorite thing about my friend: _____

_____

Recipe:

FROM THE KITCHEN OF: _____

· NOTES / TIPS ·

SERVINGS:

PREP / COOK TIME:

PREHEAT OVEN:

· INGREDIENTS ·

· DIRECTIONS ·

_____

_____

_____

_____

_____

_____

_____

_____

_____

_____

_____

_____

_____

_____

About my Friend

How we met: _____

_____

How long we've known each other: _____

What's special about this recipe: _____

_____

A favorite memory with my friend: _____

_____

My favorite thing about my friend: _____

_____

Recipe:

FROM THE KITCHEN OF: _____

SERVINGS:

PREP / COOK TIME:

PREHEAT OVEN:

· NOTES / TIPS ·

· INGREDIENTS ·

· DIRECTIONS ·

_____
_____
_____
_____
_____
_____
_____
_____
_____
_____
_____
_____
_____
_____

About my Friend

How we met: _____
_____

How long we've known each other: _____
What's special about this recipe: _____
_____

A favorite memory with my friend: _____
_____
_____

My favorite thing about my friend: _____
_____

Recipe: _____

FROM THE KITCHEN OF: _____

SERVINGS:

PREP / COOK TIME:

PREHEAT OVEN:

· NOTES / TIPS ·

· INGREDIENTS ·

· DIRECTIONS ·

_____
_____
_____
_____
_____
_____
_____
_____
_____
_____
_____
_____
_____

About my Friend

How we met: _____
_____

How long we've known each other: _____

What's special about this recipe: _____
_____

A favorite memory with my friend: _____
_____
_____

My favorite thing about my friend: _____
_____

Recipe: _____

FROM THE KITCHEN OF: _____

SERVINGS:

PREP / COOK TIME:

PREHEAT OVEN:

· NOTES / TIPS ·

_____
_____
_____
_____
_____
_____
_____

· INGREDIENTS ·

_____ _____
_____ _____
_____ _____
_____ _____
_____ _____
_____ _____

"There are three things that you should know about me. One, my friends are the most important thing in my life. Two, I never lie. And three, I make the best oatmeal raisin cookies in the world...Oh I don't make them a lot because it's not fair to the other cookies.

—Phoebe

· DIRECTIONS ·

_____

_____

_____

_____

_____

_____

_____

_____

_____

_____

_____

_____

_____

About my Friend

How we met: _____

_____

How long we've known each other: _____

What's special about this recipe: _____

_____

A favorite memory with my friend: _____

_____

My favorite thing about my friend: _____

_____

Recipe: _____

FROM THE KITCHEN OF: _____

· NOTES / TIPS ·

SERVINGS:

PREP / COOK TIME:

PREHEAT OVEN:

· INGREDIENTS ·

· DIRECTIONS ·

_____

_____

_____

_____

_____

_____

_____

_____

_____

_____

_____

_____

_____

About my Friend

How we met: _____

_____

How long we've known each other: _____

What's special about this recipe: _____

_____

A favorite memory with my friend: _____

_____

_____

My favorite thing about my friend: _____

_____

Recipe: _____

FROM THE KITCHEN OF: _____

· NOTES / TIPS ·

SERVINGS: _____

PREP / COOK TIME: _____

PREHEAT OVEN: _____

· INGREDIENTS ·

· DIRECTIONS ·

_____

_____

_____

_____

_____

_____

_____

_____

_____

_____

_____

_____

_____

_____

About my Friend

How we met: _____

_____

How long we've known each other: _____

What's special about this recipe: _____

_____

A favorite memory with my friend: _____

_____

_____

My favorite thing about my friend: _____

_____

Recipe: _____

FROM THE KITCHEN OF: _____

· NOTES / TIPS ·

SERVINGS:

PREP / COOK TIME:

PREHEAT OVEN:

· INGREDIENTS ·

· DIRECTIONS ·

_____

_____

_____

_____

_____

_____

_____

_____

_____

_____

_____

_____

_____

_____

About my Friend

How we met: _____

_____

How long we've known each other: _____

What's special about this recipe: _____

_____

A favorite memory with my friend: _____

_____

_____

My favorite thing about my friend: _____

_____

Recipe:

FROM THE KITCHEN OF: _____

SERVINGS:

PREP / COOK TIME:

PREHEAT OVEN:

· NOTES / TIPS ·

· INGREDIENTS ·

_____

_____

_____

_____

_____

_____

_____

_____

_____

_____

_____

_____

_____

About my Friend

How we met: _____

_____

How long we've known each other: _____

What's special about this recipe: _____

_____

A favorite memory with my friend: _____

_____

_____

My favorite thing about my friend: _____

_____

F·R·I·E·N·D·S
The Television Series

INSIGHTS
an imprint of

INSIGHT EDITIONS

www.insighteditions.com

MANUFACTURED IN CHINA

10 9 8 7 6 5 4 3 2 1

· RECIPE CARDS ·

Use these recipe cards to share your own recipes with friends.

Recipe: _____

F·R·I·E·N·D·S

FROM THE KITCHEN OF: _____

· INGREDIENTS ·

SERVINGS:

PREP / COOK
TIME:

PREHEAT
OVEN:

Recipe: _____

F·R·I·E·N·D·S

FROM THE KITCHEN OF: _____

· INGREDIENTS ·

SERVINGS:

PREP / COOK
TIME:

PREHEAT
OVEN:

·DIRECTIONS·

_____

_____

_____

_____

_____

_____

_____

_____

_____

_____

_____

F·R·I·E·N·D·S
THE TELEVISION SERIES

·DIRECTIONS·

_____

_____

_____

_____

_____

_____

_____

_____

_____

_____

_____

F·R·I·E·N·D·S
THE TELEVISION SERIES

· RECIPE CARDS ·

Use these recipe cards to share your own recipes with friends.

·DIRECTIONS·

F·R·I·E·N·D·S
THE TELEVISION SERIES

·DIRECTIONS·

F·R·I·E·N·D·S
THE TELEVISION SERIES